PROMISES TO KEEP

promises to keep

POEMS BY

MATTHEW E. HENRY

WAYFARER BOOKS
SAN JUAN MOUNTAINS, COLORADO

WAYFARER BOOKS
SAN JUAN MOUNTAINS, COLORADO

© 2026 text by Matthew E. Henry

Wayfarer Books supports copyright. Copyright fuels creativity, encourages diverse voices, promotes free speech, and creates a vibrant culture. Thank you for buying an authorized edition of this book and for complying with copyright laws by not reproducing, scanning, or distributing any part of it in any form without permission. You are supporting writers and allowing us to continue to publish books for every reader.

All Rights Reserved
First Edition Published in 2026 by Wayfarer Books
Cover Design and Interior Design by Connor Wolfe
Cover Photography © Koshu Kunii
Cover Illustration © Saint Benedict the African (2020, United States)
by Virginia S. Benedicte - Public Domain.
Altered by Connor Wolfe using Adobe Firefly AI, 2025.
TRADE PAPERBACK   978-1-965320-86-0
EBOOK   978-1-965320-86-0

10   9   8   7   6   5   4   3   2   1

WHOLESALE INQUIRIES? You can find our books available via Ingram, offered with standard trade terms and lifetime returnability. With printing bases in the US, the EU, the UK, and Australia, Wayfarer has the capability to fulfill orders globally. Our titles are available wherever books are sold in paperback, ebook, and audiobook. Find our books at local Indies, Bookshop.org, iTunes, Barnes & Noble, Amazon > US & International, or direct at wayfarerbookstore.com.

WAYFARERBOOKS.ORG
WAYFARERMAGAZINE.COM
WAYFARERBOOKSTORE.COM

For Rachel (TB)

Wherever you are.

CONTENTS

xv   the prophet receives the Call

I.

3   the prophet reads Asher Lev

4   the prophet explains The Day of the Lord

5   the prophet explains *Habakkuk* chapter one

6   taking off his shoes

7   the prophet's daughter begins to see

8   the reverend considers his brother, the prophet

9   the prophet is interviewed after his arrest for attempting to walk naked across the border in protest of immigration policies

10   the prophet is interviewed after his arraignment for "the malicious destruction of police property"

11   the prophet's wife finds his glasses in the freezer, again

12   self-fulfilling

13   the prophet's wife confesses to her son

14   YHWH ruminates behind the prophet

II.

19	the prophet counts the cost
20	the prophet's wife considers her role
21	the prophet calls his wife from prison after attempting to light a small satchel of kerosene-soaked money on fire and stuff it down the pants of a televangelist at a book signing
22	the prophet's wife folds the laundry
23	the prophet has his three minutes before the school board, is led out in cuffs
25	the prophet prepares an oracle while streaming his son's favorite playlist
27	YHWH withholds the vision
28	lamentations
29	the prophet's wife: her last day in church
31	the prophet's wife: excerpts from her journal in the months before she asks him to leave
33	the prophet recalculates
34	YHWH prepares a brief

III.

39   wandering, the prophet remembers summer camp

40   when the center cannot hold

41   the prophet floats along the Chebar

42   at the Babylon Street Shelter, down by the river

43   excerpts from the session notes of prophet's court ordered therapy

44   the prophet laments his colleagues

45   the prophet weighs his options

46   587 BCE

47   the prophet suffers a stroke

48   YHWH reveals His heart

IV.

53 the big fish dreams of the prophet

54 the prophet dreams a dream

55 the prophet receives another 72-hour psych hold after accosting the senator

56 the song of Miriam

57 *hannevi'ah*

58 the prophet dreams of Chris Rock

59 the prophet meets his brother at a pub

60 the prophet questions the rainbow

61 the prophet, seeing her car in the driveway, knocks on the front door, and waits

62 the prophet considers retirement

63 the prophet speaks against Rilke

64 the prophet's wife explains to her daughter, in part, why she returned his keys

65 the prophet's daughter: excerpts from her diary, in the months before her brother's death

66 apobaterion: a place of landing

67 the prophet's wife considers "the repressed Mother"

68 YHWH tries to explain

CODA

73   the prophet dreams of being Called again

Acknowledgments
Notes
About the Author
About the Publisher

the prophet receives the Call

and the word of the LORD came to _____ saying, mortal,
you tell those ungrateful, orphaned bastards I rescued
from the roadside, I've had enough of their bullshit.
I swear by Myself, I won't be moved. won't be talked down
from the ledge they've built on the edge of My grace.
no number of righteous friends will restrain My right arm
from cursing the ground beneath their feet. the day of reckoning
has arrived.

tell those trifling sons of bitches My nostrils flare
with the stench of burnt offerings rising from their altars
of strange fire. tell them I see how they strut like whores
from one john to the next, sating every assorted evil—
appetites without innocence's blush. tell them how I kept
holding back My wrath for the love of them and My good name—
mercies pillared like the foundations of the earth—but
those motherfuckers never learn. don't know when to quit.
don't care about the brother-blood bleating like slaughtered sheep
from the red-sodden earth. tell them they shouldn't rest,
but be assured that it will be investigated and answered in kind.

tell those comfortably callous assholes when My destroyers
ride on pale-green horses, no "x" will mark where their cities
once stood. no stone will be left atop another. no wisp of grain
seed will remain, nor any mother's youngest son. tell them
that they will know that *I Am*—the LORD their God—
is officially not fucking around.

I

Sometimes I pray: please don't speak

"Dein allererstes Wort war: Licht,"
—Ranier Maria Rilke

the prophet reads Asher Lev

the LORD has spoken. what is there but to scream
in a special way, laugh in the special way visiting angels
never suspect. to blaze bone-fuel from marrow
to skin. to see between thin spaces with eyes attuned
to the sacred simplicity altar-ed in daily life: bread
and water, sex and cartoons. *every trade has her whores,*
you said. but this is no easy trick: an apprenticeship
for grasping a mantle of stars, sewing a waistcoat
of wind with calloused fingers, attempting to clothe
naked children content and bound only by certain
death. perhaps we're all sixty seconds away from salvation,
soft reprieves convincing us religion's still a dream
worth dreaming. a holy reclamation project—the artist,
the poet, the preacher, searching for lies that scan well.

the prophet explains *The Day of the Lord*

it's like asking the sun to fall out of the sky,
the moon to suddenly explode.

it's like the old story: a man hides from a lion
in the cave of a sleeping bear. he flees
the rousing growls into a crumbling cabin nearby.
when he doubles over—palms pressed
against a wall—he's bitten by the owner's
abandoned pet viper.

it's like waiting in line at a club and learning
the bouncer is your older brother.
you're ready to push beyond the velvet rope,
past the pretty, pretentious jerks obsessed
with their fits and phones. ready for their heads
to jerk up in horror as you breeze by,
their faces flickering like oil lamps.
but your brother knows you'll get
not-enough-to black-out, but
just-enough-to-make-everyone-regret-knowing-you
drunk and thrown out for placing your hands
and tongue everywhere they should not be.
so it's your face—road-rashed and bleeding—
that ends up kissing the side
of the vomit-covered dumpster
in the alley out back.

the prophet explains *Habakkuk* chapter one

a kindergartner is playing with a cherished toy
she brought from home. the class bully knocks
her to the ground, snatching the toy, scraping
her knees. she fights back. they struggle.
there are pinches, kicks. a third child scrambles
to the oaken desk to tell Teacher. He already knows,
has been watching. ears filled with the sound
of carpet burns and pulled hair, the tattletale
wonders why He makes no move to stop it,
why meanness is allowed to continue unchecked.
eventually, dusting chalk from pants, the Teacher
stands, walks past the bloodying children, and lifts
the classroom phone. after a mumble, He returns
to His desk, folds hands in His lap, and begins to hum.
unable to withstand the strain, the complainer asks,
"why aren't You doing anything? who did You call?"
the Teacher cooly explains He phoned the high school.
they are sending two 12th graders with a history of violence
to break the toy and rape the fighting children.

taking off his shoes

every night i pray
He didn't choose me
for my readiness
to hear desert voices,
my ability to turn
and see
      nothing
more than
what heatstroke
and dehydration
can conjure,
yet continue
calling it *faith*.

the prophet's daughter begins to see

my father is a goldfish
overfed with purpose,
bloated by divinity.

every morning i awake
afraid
to check his bowl.

the reverend considers his brother, the prophet

while he didn't murder my sons for "strange fire,"
the Sunday morning slaughter of my congregation was enough.
his flint words offering only offense, no conviction.

he thinks i erect altars to a God of gold and glory
for those who don't know the price of bread and milk
outside of an election year. he may be right.

but he won't face the other truth. there is safety shouting
his jeremiads from outside communal walls—it's easy
to condemn when not sharing blood Sabbath after Sabbath.

**the prophet is interviewed after his arrest
for attempting to walk naked across the border
in protest of immigration policies**

i was cold
but so are they

the prophet is interviewed after his arraignment for "the malicious destruction of police property"

shall we bask in the irony, the ugliness
of the charges? *malicious destruction* when
a man was lynched yesterday? a child
of God whose empty hands will never
again hold a son to the chest red-cratered
by exit wounds?
                                       so yes,
i plastered every patrol car's windshield
and window with an industrial grade adhesive
and the black and white reminder—
a man was lynched yesterday—
                                       lest they forget.

the prophet's wife finds his glasses in the freezer, again

he forgets Deborah:

the only tree steadfast
in the weald of shivering men,
wisdom hung from her branches.

she who must mother Barak—
send him out, hold his hand,
bring him to a dry place
in silence—knowing the time
to speak, to summon liquid spears
and spades to bury those who
would touch the apple of His eye.

Deborah whose song names no husband.

self-fulfilling

You
are clothed in the vastness of mountains,
robed in fiery desert winds. pillars of cloud
and sea salt gird Your loins,

                                        while i attempt
contentment with dust, ashes,
and sacrificed skins. all i have is less than

You seem aware:
                      this bag of words,
this failing vision, these arms weighed down
by the effort of raising flesh. i stumble
within this uneasy alliance with breath

You consider a daily mercy.

the prophet's wife confesses to her son

i shook him once.
grabbed him by the shoulders
as he stepped out of the shower.

my nails drew blood.

his eyes were visionary wide.
i slapped the left side of his face dry
and asked him
how much is enough?

he didn't answer.

YHWH ruminates behind the prophet

how lonely are the feet of him who brings My news.
when small talk turns to religion and politics,
who will keep their stool, listen with more than pity,
buy him a beer? nobody loves the host inquiring about
the reservation you couldn't be bothered to call in advance.
the fool you imagine a king, striding through tables
of his importance—twenties stuffed in greased palms—,
barely makes enough to feed the children who stumble
from apartment-close corners, their empty bowls acclaiming
his failures, his wife's glare nightly dimming his merit.
My poor son tires of walking into the solitude of My greatness
without a hand to hold. tires of eyes lifted, never straight.
I weep for him and all that comes next.

II

*"... when did I assume such a burden?
Where did I sign on God's dotted line?
With my mother's milk. With inviable ink."*

–The Nakedness of the Fathers, ALICIA SUSKIN OSTRIKER

the prophet counts the cost

i aspire to be loved less than Abraham. Abraham
who was found worthy of losing his first son
long before the binding of the one who—
like God—never spoke to him again. Isaac
only returned at Ishmael's request
to bury him. estranged from both boys,
Abraham went into the earth with one ear
always tilted. he startled at every sound, joy
immediately soured. he strained to hear
what he thought was a friend. the Voice
from so long ago. the Whisper that ceased
before the ram's cinders went cold.

the prophet's wife considers her role

sometimes i forget my name.
it seems "one flesh" means
we are him. and yet it falls to me
to encourage him. to seal his covenant
as if by circumcision—an action
outside my body. a word without meaning.

but like Zipporah, i wield the knife.
cut to save him—our daughter,
our son—from an inactive Father,
at whose feet i'd throw the remainder.

the prophet calls his wife from prison after attempting to light a small satchel of kerosene-soaked money on fire and stuff it down the pants of a televangelist at a book signing

the zeal of His house
assaulted me
again

the prophet's wife folds the laundry

he forgets Huldah:

to whom all men—
of regal robe, of priestly tassel—
ran and bowed the knee.

she who they roused
from Torah study and begged
to hold YHWH's hand
back another generation.

he forgets Jeremiah and Zechariah,
were left outside in the dark.

the prophet has his three minutes before the school board, is led out in cuffs

privileged is the two-year fiefdom allowing you to break the spirit of a child.

privileged is the comfort you take in a 15-year-old mourning her desire to simply be in her own body.

privileged is the arrogance inherent in your refusal to honor her meek request of a pronoun change on forms that don't concern you.

privileged is the fullness of your bellies with the books you hunger and thirst to burn, your vomitous mouths smirked with fricative slurs.

privileged is the small mercy of never being asked your birth-gender as you enter a bathroom, or your genitals being carded outside the locker room of a sport someone attempts to ban you from playing.

privileged is you seeing God so clearly, your heart is pure enough to ask grown-ass adults to death threat her home, their children to throw glass bottles at her head in the cafeteria and between classes.

privileged is your child's prom dress never going viral on right-wing social media, being blown up and scrutinized by a klan of mouth-breathing douchebags searching for a bulge.

privileged is your fucked up belief that you're persecuted by her
mere presence, her uppity lack of silence in the face of your hatred—
the supposed stench of her speech offending your righteousness,
rising to the heavens.

rejoice and be glad! great is your reward on earth, but not in heaven.
the LORD has reserved a special place for you away from the
invented evils you prophesy against. your eternal retirement home
will always be warmer than the southern sensibilities you claim. I
hope you get used to the smell—more rotten than your souls.

world without end.

the prophet prepares an oracle while streaming his son's favorite playlist

they have rejected the instruction of the Lord,
have not kept His statutes. but it's hard
to be a spiritual being when shit is shaking
what you believe in. living in turbulent times—
the blind leading the blind—they have been led astray
by the same lies after which their ancestors walked.
somebody told me it's the end of the world,
but that's just for some: those who trample
the heads of the poor into the dust of the earth,
who push the afflicted out of the way.
thus says the Lord,

> *when worst comes to worst,*
> *My people come first.*

thus says the Lord,

> *ya'll gonna keep fucking around*
> *with Me and turn Me back*
> *to the old Me.*

does a bird fall into a snare when there is no trap?
does a snare spring up from the ground with nothing in it?
thus says the Lord,

> *as the shepherd rescues two legs*
> *or a piece of an ear*
> *from the mouth of the lion,*
> *I'm about to ruin the image*
> *and the style that you're used to.*

thus says the Lord,

> *if you preach hate at the service,*
> *those words aren't anointed.*
> *that holy water that you soak in*
> *has been poisoned.*

is a trumpet blown in a city and the people are not afraid?
does disaster befall a city unless the Lord has done it?
thus says the Lord,

> *seek Me and live!*
> *let justice roll down like water*
> *and righteousness*
> *like an ever-flowing stream.*

I take day as a blessing and see the night as a lesson,
twilight as a message for me to write a confession.
but they do not know how to do right.
thus says the Lord,

> *to those who store up violence*
> *and robbery in their strongholds,*
> *I will send the cosmic schadenfreude*
> *of only meeting your Creator*
> *on the day you are destroyed.*
> *I will tear down the winter house,*
> *and the summer house,*
> *and the houses of ivory shall perish,*
> *and the great houses*
> *shall come to an end.*

YHWH withholds the vision

 tomorrow, hand in hand, mother
and her child will cut covenant
at a crosswalk, with eye contact,
a nod, and a grateful wave.

impatience will swerve around,
extent a middle finger to the yielding
driver, and crumple the pair
into a *pieta*.

lamentations

how empty sits the room once filled with his laughter.
how like a womb scrapped clean it has become. a city
of exile. an utter desolation. i close the door behind me.

the weeping of his sister—cutting through our walls
like a knife through the throat—is matched only by
his mother's screams. how the Lord has made her suffer.

this grief envelopes. barbed wire around the heart,
a plastic bag over the head. bitterness churns my stomach
to bile on the bathroom floor.

but the Lord is good to those who wait for Him
in silence, mouths filled with dirt. His compassion
will not be absent forever. His mercies will lift the weight
crushing precious things when the unseen is accomplished.

today she will not be comforted.

the prophet's wife: her last day in church

after all we sacrificed,
You heard her prayers?
rescued the son of a mother
who takes You more seriously
than You do Yourself?
how am I allowed less?

and now, as my better boy
fills the womb of the earth,
i must listen to her praise You,
speak of Your loving-kindness,
Your grace-filled mercies,
grasp her hand, receive her pity,
and lie amens?

as she opens Your book
and reads of the comfort
she says i should seek
in Your presence,
as she presents the false assurances
of a preoccupied father
concerned less with his child's cries
than a business meeting
later that morning,
i am expected

*to restrain my hands
from her face, her neck,
as Yours remain
regrettably out of reach?*

the prophet's wife: excerpts from her journal in the months before she asks him to leave

. . .he says i'm too sensitive. get too worked up, too hysterical about his images. "they're only metaphors," he says. "only." it's amazing that a man filled with so much compassion, remains so blind. damsels in distress, pimps and whores, and all his other unfaithful abuses of power. as if life and death are not held on the tips of tongues.

. . . i've learned to ignore the phone calls from my sisters and the few friends i have left. the "i'm so sorry"s and "are you okay"s after seeing his latest blaze on the local news. i have wine. and our daughter. at least i know where he is, what he's doing. that he's still alive. it's nice to know where i can go to see the passion those eyes once held for me.

. . . so distracted by his "divine duty." i wonder if Gomer needed the warmth so often absent our bed: the need to feel her spine pressed against another's chest at night, to hear the grunts of real or feigned love from a stranger because her husband was otherwise occupied and forgetful as God.

... fuckfuckfuckfuckfuckfuck fuckfuckfuckfuckfuckfuck fuckfuckfuckfuckfuckfuckfuckfuckYOU...

… i remember reading Frost's "Home Burial" in high school, finding the story both familiar and foreign. how the sudden outburst of emotions, following a prolonged silence, reminded me of my parents and their many miscommunications. an adult tragedy I found interesting, but did not fully understand. but now, hearing the concern he attempts to wrap around my shoulders with his questions, while knowing he is incapable of simply seeing me …

… i'm not sure which of them i hate more. i should be ashamed of this, but i'm not…

the prophet recalculates

so You are the One
who comes after

fathers inherit
the early bloom

of wilted sons.
You whose caring

is a nightmare.
whose stone voice

crushes all sounds—
the pleading of lips

lost in the endless
gulf between us—

knowing my
beloved child

will never become
a man, an aging man,

an aged man. so
are You then my heir?

YHWH prepares a brief

Jeremiah indicted Me for inaction, breech of contract.
openly mocked My innocence and deigned to pass
judgment, knowing the grand jury was already rigged,
the fix in my favor. but I let him get it off his chest.

Job's lengthy subpoena compelled My appearance.
He alternately cast Me as defendant, prosecutor,
defense counsel, and judge. but when I took the stand…
what outcome could he have been expecting?

Isaiah—My suffering servant—filed a class action
lawsuit on behalf of his people, demanded redress
for the double portion punishment, he argued, surpassed
the crime. I patiently reached for the codes I had written.

at least John—who studied at his father's feet, before
his own were baptizing wet—learned from their example.
had the good sense to keep his mouth shut, not lose his head
with Me before they came and took it off his shoulders.

III

*"First you created longing,
then later earth and heaven.
And a home for us? No. Not yet!"*

– "At Dusk," ABRAHAM J. HESCHEL

wandering, the prophet remembers summer camp

as we apply our hands to their crafts—
lanyards and wooden trinkets only a mother
could love—give us the strength to sit
around their fires and mouth their songs,
while our hearts babble with the rivers of home,
found at the foot of Your mountain. as we lay
beneath unfamiliar stars in synthetic fleece,
we pray our Mother-tongued letters will assure:
the weeks will pass, the scrapes will mend,
the ivy's poison will be salved. until the wooden gates
lift up their heads and Your sliding-door chariot comes
with a peal of horn, making straight the highway home,
we wait. we wait to be held to Your Bosom, we wait
for You, the great homesickness we could never shake off,

when the center cannot hold

before the ambulance arrived,
her stillness was an open grave
between them.

she will find no comfort in the groceries
bursting the cupboards—payment
for the small room he rents.

she believed him a hope, a talisman,
a direct line to My Healing,
despite all appearances.

he was her last unanswered prayer.
she wonders whose sin made him fail
her, her son.

now her husband retains soul custody
in the home his stroke built
two years before.

her third eye blinks
to the medicine cabinet—
the fare to join her family.

the prophet floats along the Chebar

beyond the bill and empty plate, knives
are aggressively arranged against *ersatz* walls.
forks become battering rams. spoons loaded
with pennies are poised as catapults.
it's a siege-worthy circle. she clears these first.

in the center, packets of jelly and jam preserves
are bricked, their roof tiled with sugar packets.
toothpicks and a straw-wrapper twist into a tree
planted beside a pepper-grained garden, framed
by a picket fence of salt. a nice touch, she thought.
admired more than his 10% tip.

she couldn't help but notice how much it looked—
from a certain angle—like a happy home.
once the table has been scraped bare, she wished
she had pulled our her phone, taken a picture.

at the Babylon Street Shelter, down by the river

whose children must i dash against the rocks,
sledgehammer with the righteous indignation
of the oppressed?
                          You brought me here, left me
in this strange land. i am alone for raising my voice.
for singing Your songs. for not forgetting.

                          You are my Tormentor,
the Devastator of my family.

where is my double revenge? which of Your children
may i destroy for all You've done to me? is this
Your answer— here in this splintering mirror?
in the blood pooling at my feet?

excerpts from the session notes of the prophet's court-ordered therapy

...our conversations read like an unfinished O'Connor novel. i half expect him to scream of baptism and redemption, oversexed girls and drowned deficients...

... a ragged figure vigorously swings through the backwoods of his mind: a vaguely embodied telos he cannot escape...

...he feels a wisdom in his blood: the reason for everything he believes will happen, no matter what is done to keep happenings at bay. for him there is truly no peace for the redeemed. and therein may lie his integrity...

... no doubt this all stems from the father-figure he won't discuss ...

the prophet laments his colleagues

brothers, we've lost all our mystics.

your voices have been silenced by
a secular imbalance of clozapine
& lithium. alignment with Insight
dulled by drips of thorazine & haldol.
eyes no longer hear, ears cannot see
all that is written on the heart
of the sky, the longing of the wind,
the burning wheels of locust &
scrolls of honey budding like rods.

the unpierced side of Ecstasy screams.

after my hour-long, forced meditation
with the false prophets of strange fire,
i see you shuffle through a wilderness
of antiseptic halls—blue robed, but aimless,
anxious—, bound to beds by white straps,
or seated, staring into thin spaces. i admire
how, in their presence, you can blankly pretend
not to hear the Voice of warning:

the descent of disasters unimagined.

the prophet weighs his options

- ignore The Call and wait for His punishment
- flee to another country, under His wrathful eye and long arm
- feed the maw of the storming sea my meager bones and gristle
- wait to be swallowed, molar-ed, or ingested by an enormous fish
- spend a bold day behind ethnic enemy lines in the middle of a race war, hoping i get capped or catch a stray
- deliver outrageous, incendiary lies to said enemies, hoping i incite their rage, or God's
- shit-talk God when none of the above works
- beg God to kill me
- ignore God—again—when He tries to comfort me
- beseech God—emphatically—to just fucking kill me

587 BCE

at some point
pressure builds,
an 18¢ shunt
forgets to open
or close, and
it's all over
in a quiet cloud
of Jack Kennedy
whiplash—back
and to the left.

the prophet suffers a stroke

"the piano has been drinking, not me." —Tom Waits

this is the temple of the Lord! serve leaven
bread made with human hair for violence
is scribbled on hearts like crayon on closet
walls or a failed father watching his daughters
whore themselves on a nationally syndicated
shock-show broadcast from the seven hills above
a graveyard's lonesome valley a jazz club filled
with drying bones where ribcages sound like
Stevie Wonder playing clavinet for widows
and infants starving on ivory beds but this is
the temple of the LORD! where my tongue
was touched by hot coals and Jerry Falwell killed
the Baptist brand like roadside bombers at abortion
clinics and Uriah lying dead at my feet God sits
in the witness stand hand on a Bible dancing
to beat a trumped-up charge with only transatlantic slaves,
Vincent Chin, and wage-gapped women as character
witnesses and while the adulterer hires an advocate
for the other woman i sit and pray and ask how long
this is the temple of the LORD?

YHWH reveals His heart

you read this and think I Am cruel,
uncaring in universal administration.
that I miss sparrows, miscount the hairs

remaining on My servant's head—
the last thread he clings to. you think
he is another in a long line of prophets

who must cleave tendon from bone,
abandon family to embrace Me fully.
that no prophet has ever returned

whole, if they ever returned, if home
remained at all. it's true. not all received
chariots, but all were honored in My way.

it was a mercy I took Moses, held him to
My breast. his eyes would never see
how red promised clay could become.

I stopped Ezekiel from all his heart
would regret giving voice. time enough to see
he would never want his wife beside him

in Babylon—no place for their unborn children.
Samuel and Daniel, Hosea and Jeremiah…for all
I graciously turned My head, pretending

not to notice the small solace taken—the slight
curve of lips—when they understood, when
in time they saw, that I also lost a Son.

IV

"Forgive him."

—"on Slow Learning," Scott Cairns

the big fish dreams of the prophet

i remember the Call to travel leagues outside my currents,
to head east until i knew. the confusion of my pod, my husband, my son,
at my hurried departure. my insistence i must make this journey alone.

it was 40 days before submerging beneath the sudden storm,
then sudden calm. then the human slowly falling towards me—
smiling—until i rose to cradle him in my mouth, as i knew
i should. for three days i circled, holding his violent maelstrom
within, forced to fast and pray and wait for his final song
of peace. eventually i was led to a coast farther east, farther north,
where i left him coughing on the shore—his face a stone curse—
and headed for home.

the prophet dreams a dream

he's an ox grazing beside the field
he ploughed an hour before.
drenched with dew, hair tangled
with white feathers, twigs,
freshly trampled stalks of grain—
the food of the Master, His servants,
and invited guests—
he's finally at peace.

                      but he is not content.
there is a compulsion, an instinct
for his eyes to rise, to shake
his woolen head clear. to finish

the prophet receives another 72-hour psych hold after accosting the senator

when quiet, the destitute are invisible.

[he wasn't noticed
sitting on the stone steps
outside her office
until he grabbed her face—
palms cupping her cheeks,
fingers wrapping her occipital ridge.
nose denting her temple,
he whispered in her ear
before staggering back,
as if collapsing
under a great weight
or being relieved of one.]

                                                at least
this is how her security detail explained the lapse
in threat assessment and response time. they made
up for it with a rib-bruising tackle, an arm-twisted
restraint, and knees on his back and neck during
an invasive search for weapons, which yielded only
a desiccated Bible and wallet empty of all but
an expired driver's license and a yellowing photo
of a boy.

the song of Miriam

the prophet's instructions were clear.

she sat on the edge of the fountain—
a horse and rider raised above the sea
of copper hopes lost beneath the water
now melting her leather soles
to leprous skin.

40 minutes he said. time enough
for their cameras to capture
Jesus loves me, this i know and the other
Sunday school songs she thought forgotten
on her congressional rise. news at 11. they wish
she had a tambourine, a Bible. she thumps
her chest instead, feeling the hum—
the change—three weeks after receiving
her secret oncologist's second opinion.

hannevi'ah

that night, in the calm of her office, she heard…

on a large legal pad she began to conceive—
in all caps—an answer. began to birth a plan
for the land of both her people—so long
spoiled and savaged, so long carried away
like prey in the mouths of rabid nations,
near and far.

she thinks she has the support. has faith
she can leverage the myriad favors she's owed.
they will call her naïve, but she feels possibility
in her breast. this time, she believes the children
of Abraham—
    Ishamel, her mother;
        Isaac, her father—
may hear God,
    may hear the laughter
        of God, among them.

the prophet dreams of Chris Rock

it is finished. get up and go home.

*sorry brother, He no longer answers
with fire. ain't no clouds parting. no
androgenous white angels descending
with glad tidings of sacrifice affirmed.*

*don't give me that woe-is-me, looking
like an arrow-riddled martyr shit. you knew
what He was about, what you signed up for.
you've kept your head. all your teeth
are still in your mouth. be happy
you're still breathing.*

*what? do you want a cookie? credit?
you one of those people expecting praise
for doing the shit you was supposed to do?
fuck outta here with your ignorant ass,
you low expectation having motherfucker.
it's your kind that makes us all look bad.*

*what you do next is not my problem.
I don't know what to tell you man.
like you, I'm just a messenger—
take it up with Management.
I have other stops to make tonight.*

the prophet meets his brother at a pub

five minutes every century
the eye of the Whirlwind
passes over
and there is peace—

the sentry sees
nothing
the horizon is clear

fruit ripens on the vine
the branch fears no flame

the vulture weeps

the prophet questions the rainbow

inverted weapon strung in dirt, hung

on invisible pegs—empty of your promise—

do you point toward friend or foe?

the prophet, seeing her car in the driveway, knocks on the front door, and waits

after months of feeding the Tishbite—bread

and meat from some celestial store, or stolen

from the sills of those deemed worthy

to go without—what happened to the ravens?

when the brooks ran dry, when the cabinets

and cisterns went bare, were the helpers—

darker than doves or sparrows—remembered

for their obedience, their love, or simply left to fall?

the prophet considers retirement

all he ever wanted was a respite from mountains.

a cabin in the woods beside a still voice of brook.

a place where trees remain silent. rods remain rods.

all he ever wanted was to deliver the message

and return whole. to prepare a meal without wings

dipped in death. to smile with his wife, comfort

his children when they wake and, after a day

of twice-long miles, sleep beside his fathers.

the prophet speaks against Rilke

i am too much in the world

to make each hour holy— too small

to be in Your presence simply.

i know my will and with hushed movements

draw namelessly away from Your immensity

too weak, too old to bear the tonnage

of Your image, Your praise

or Joban consideration. i want to unfold

in a closed space, clear of Your sight—

to describe myself in detail: a darkened cityscape;

a pimpled daughter; an iced glass of beer; a barge

towing nothing but itself across a placid bay.

the prophet's wife explains to her daughter, in part, why she returned his keys

Ezekiel was warned

he would be blinded—

the light of his eyes snatched—

and was forbidden to grieve

for her.

it was how stoic your father stood

over his little grave—the way i imagined

Zeke hovered over his wife's too soon tomb—

that made me think he knew,

conjured mount moriah in his mind,

and did nothing to stop it.

i choose now to believe i was wrong.

the prophet's daughter: excerpts from her diary, the month before her brother's death

…i've been sitting in this sterile basement for days—trying to find the meaning of life, or at least meaning for right now—when it occurred to me: i fear a life folded into a gold binding, buried on a dusty bookshelf, waiting for some lost soul to skip the introduction, read from page 5 to 387, sigh, and then sit down to soak in my moral, before switching on the weather…

…father, i'd give a penny for what you've got on your mind, but such trust cannot be bought. no one tells the doctor the whole truth in a checkup— there's too much history for a 5 min conversation in cold hands, mostly filled with awkward silence…

…Old Man, if we had time to breathe we'd choke on our own air…

… i just finished the book of Ecclesiastes. God promises life will be hell and the world will suck, but we should follow Him until the end, because that's the only thing worthwhile. eat, drink, and enjoy life while you can. and fight cynicism. out of this story of unrequited love i get to learn how to love deeply, live passionately, and gain wisdom…

…maybe it's not any big revelation i've come to. it's not that i've grown up. maybe it's simple. maybe i just fell in love with God and His little children. maybe i have to be willing to do everything before He will use me to do anything. maybe beginning to surrender myself was the best thing i have ever done…

apobaterion: a place of landing

in time he faces the flickering hearth
his daughter bought at Christmas. 80 inches
of visions he climbed no mountain to obtain.
she wanted him to relax—splurged
on the sports package, the movie classics,
the cartoon suite. she was unable to block
the 24-hour news cycle. reclining on an ark
of plush velvet—remote in one hand, 12 ounces
of refreshment in the other, enjoying the divinity
of Dolby surround sound—his callouses subside
into the belief all hope is graspable. that all stories
can end with consolation, a promise fulfilled.
but his eyes, his ears twitch, unable to agree.

the prophet's wife considers "the repressed Mother"

they tell us "there is always another interpretation."
that we are required to "turn it, turn it," for it contains
everything under, and above, the sun. i wonder.

where are Sarah's screams recorded? who awoke to find
the dent beside her cold and her boy's bed empty. she who knew
she was taken in the silence of self-righteous certainty.

she was another barren woman who cradled laughter in her arms
until her husband's doubt demanded a lesson from a God
who had never asked for a child to be sacrificed before.

they say Satan appeared to her after. in one account he lied, told her
Issac's throat had been slit. in another, that Issac had been spared.
both purport Satan knew the greatness of grief or joy would kill her.

should I not read both as a mercy?

YHWH tries to explain

it's in your best interest to believe
that I always get My way. eventually.
that none of My plans are ever thwarted,

even by free will. I know. it's all so hard
to understand. I sit on the inside
of what you call *wonder*—My counsel

hidden, My knowledge seemingly opaque,
no matter how brightly it's shined, shared
in the myriad ways you'll still call *mystery*.

I don't need to provide examples of how you feel
your world collapses—your complaints
are already top of mind, piercing My heart.

listen. really listen to what I am telling you,
more than you violently question the reasons—
and yes, there are reasons—why My plans

include suffering, but do not include suffering.
it's confusing. I know. you don't see how
I can bind both leviathan and behemoth

yet cannot restrain their terror. I don't need
your repentance in dust or ashes, the blood
of first-born sons or daughters dashed

like hope against the rocks of circumstance.
within My control, there are many things
outside of My control. even Job—eventually—

was able to see this, admit this. at least I hope so.
our relationship was never quite the same. we never
spoke again. but we all have to make sacrifices.

CODA

*"For last year's words belong to last year's language
And next year's words await another voice."*

– *Four Quartets*, T.S. ELIOT

the prophet dreams of being Called again

and when Moses was a hundred and twenty-one years old,
    after leading his flock from the backside of the desert,
to tents west of the Jordan at the foot of the mountain of God
    (his eyes still bright, his force strong as seven teams of oxen),
the angel of the LORD appeared as a raven beside a flowering bush
    a thousand cubits from his tent in Canaan.

and when the LORD saw that he turned left and right,
    searching for Aaron or Miriam, Joshua or Caleb,
He called unto him from the beak of the bird:
    Moses.
        Moses!

but Moses backed away, slowly, eyes closed, fists balled to his ears.
    I am not here, he whispered.
        I am not here.

ACKNOWLEDGMENTS

Every poem in this collection contains direct quotations, references, and allusions to images, events, and characters found in the Hebrew Bible (and a tiny bit of the Christian New Testament) intentionally and subconsciously. To save us all considerable pain, I only include a handful of the most significant references, other relevant notes, and my immense gratitude to the magazines and journals that first published earlier versions of these poems.

- "'the prophet reads Asher Lev" employs phrases from the novel *My Name is Asher Lev* by Chaim Potok and a line from "Is It True?" by Anne Sexton.

- "the prophet is interviewed after his arraignment for 'the malicious destruction of police property'" references the "A Man Was Lynched Yesterday" flag that was flown outside the national headquarters of the NAACP from 1936-1938 following the September 6th lynching of A.L. McCamy in Dalton, GA. Various versions of the flag have continued into the present for obvious reasons.

- "YHWH ruminates behind the prophet" is after Gwendolyn Brooks poem "The Preacher Ruminates: Behind the Sermon."

- "the prophet prepares an oracle while streaming his son's favorite playlist" is a cento of the following works (in order): Amos 2:4; "Respiration," Talib Kweli; "Clock Without Hands," The Roots; Amos 2:4; "Quicksand Millennium," The Roots; Amos 2:7; "Worst Comes to Worst," Dilated Peoples; "Forgot about Dre," Dr. Dre; Amos 3:5; Amos 3:12; "The Humpty Dance," Digital Underground; "Same Love," Macklemore; Amos 3:6; Amos 5:4; Amos 5:24; "Aquamarine," Black Thought; Amos 3:10; "Lord Intended," De La Soul; and Amos 3:15.

- "the prophet recalculates" is after Rainer Maria Rilke's poems "*Und seine Sorgfalt is tuns wie ein Alb*" and "*Du bist der Erbe.*"

- "Wandering, the prophet remembers summer camp" takes its closing line from Rilke's "*Ich liebe dich, du sanftestes Gesetz.*"

- "from the notebook of the prophet's court-ordered therapist" borrows imagery from throughout Flannery O'Connor's fiction and nonfiction. A version was first published in *Dust & Ashes* (Californios Press, 2020),

- "YHWH reveals His heart" was first published as "YHWH breaks the fourth wall" in *The Windhover.*

- The word "*hannevi'ah*" translates from Hebrew to mean "the woman prophet." It is a phrase found only in Isaiah 8:1-4, the passage after which this poem is based.

- "the prophet dreams of Chris Rock" employs lines from Chris Rock's "Niggas vs. Black People" segment of his HBO comedy special *Bring the Pain* (1996). It is also indebted to Rock's appearance in the Kevin Smith movie *Dogma*.

- "the prophet speaks against Rilke" responds to Rilke's "*Ick bin auf der Welt zu allein und doch nicht allein genug*" and was first published in *Dappled Things*

- "the prophet's daughter: excerpts from her diary, the month before her brother's death" is a found poem based on an email from Rachel.

- "the prophet's wife considers the 'repressed Mother'" is composed from reflections in Alicia Suskin Ostriker's essay "Out of my Sight: The Buried Woman in Biblical Narrative." A noteworthy sample: "Is it possible that the whole story of canonicity, the whole story of authority in our culture, is intimately bound up with the repressed Mother, shimmering and struggling at the liminal threshold of consciousness, against whom the Father must anxiously defend himself? So it appears to me."

NOTES

I am deeply grateful to Connor Wolfe and all the good people at Wayfarer Books for their time, effort, and belief in this project.

Blessing upon the writers, scholars, and musicians who were instrumental in the development of this collection, whether I've met them in real life or not: Black Thought (Tariq Luqmaan Trotter), Leslie Allen, Daniel Block, Gwendolyn Brooks, Walter Brueggemann, T.S. Eliot, Robert Frost, Wilda C. Gafney, Moshe Greenburg, Abraham J. Heschel, William Holladay, Gail Lee, Archibald MacLeish, Flannery O'Connor, Maria Ranier Rilke, Whitney Rio-Ross, J.J.M Roberts, Raymond P. Scheindlin, Daniel Smith-Christopher, Adam Sol, Carl Sandburg, Alicia Suskin Ostriker, Adele Reinhartz, Phyllis Trible, Renita Weems, and Elie Wiesel.

Many thanks to M.T. Davila, Carolyn Davis, Carole Fontaine, Mark Heim, and Gregory Mobley for their tutelage and in whose classes at Andover Newton Theological School the Prophet was born.

Special thanks to the readers and commenters on the various versions of this manuscript Jennifer Avignon, Linda Carney-Goodrich, Joel Dunlap, Frances Klien, Phil Lafountain, Kate McCann, Kayla Peterson-Neto, Annie Pluto, Mandy Smith, and Montague Williams.

Biggest thanks to Pauline and Edmund Henry: my first Sunday School teachers, practical theologians, and parents.

ABOUT THE AUTHOR

Matthew E. Henry is an educator, essayist, and occasional fiction writer. He is the author of the full-length collections *Said the Frog to the Scorpion* (2024), *The Third Renunciation* (2023), and *The Colored Page* (2022), as well as the chapbooks *Have You Heard the One About...?* (2023), *Dust & Ashes* (2020), and *Teaching While Black* (2020). He serves as editor-in-chief of *The Weight Journal* and as nonfiction editor of *Porcupine Literary*. Henry holds an MFA, an MA in theology, and a PhD in education. He writes about education, race, religion, and dismantling oppressive systems at www.MEHPoeting.com

Wayfarer Books is a fiercely independent, queer & trans-owned press publishing bold literature from the wild and societal margins.

At Wayfarer Books we believe poetry is the language of the earth. We believe words, like rivers through wild places, can change the shape of the world. We publish poets and writers and renegades who stand outside of mainstream culture; poets, essayists, and storytellers whose work might withstand the scrutiny of crows and coyotes, those who are cryptic and floral, the crepuscular, and the queer-at-heart. We are more than just a publisher but a community of writers. Our mission is to produce books that can serve as a compass and map to all wayfarers through wild terrain.

WAYFARERBOOKS.ORG

SUPPORTING INDIGENOUS FUTURES
1% GIVEN BACK

Wayfarer Books is based in the San Juan Mountains near Mesa Verde, on the lands of the Ancestral Pueblo, the Southern Ute, the Weenuche (Mountain Ute), the Diné (Navajo), and the San Juan Southern Paiute Tribe. We honor the generations of Indigenous communities who have stewarded these lands for thousands of years. We acknowledge that this place was taken through genocide, colonization, and displacement. We respect the Indigenous peoples who remain here, both past and present. As one concrete act of accountability, we are launching 1% Given Back. Beginning in 2026, we will give 1% of Wayfarer's net profits directly to the Indigenous nations on whose lands we are based, in support of sovereignty, Indigenous futures, and wealth redistribution. We do this in the belief that acknowledgment should move beyond words and into tangible practice.

learn more at wayfarerbooks.org

www.ingramcontent.com/pod-product-compliance
Lightning Source LLC
LaVergne TN
LVHW040107080526
838202LV00045B/3810